IMPORTANT BUSINESS

Office People Coloring Book

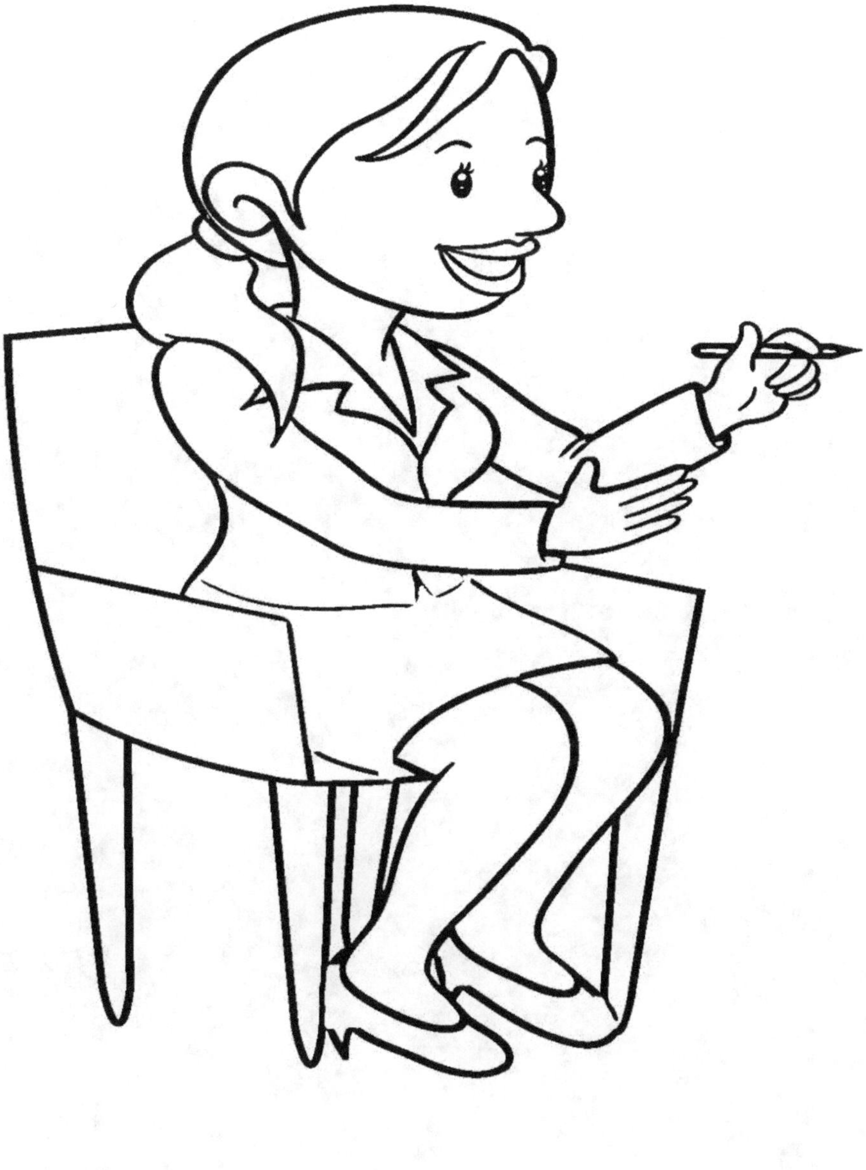

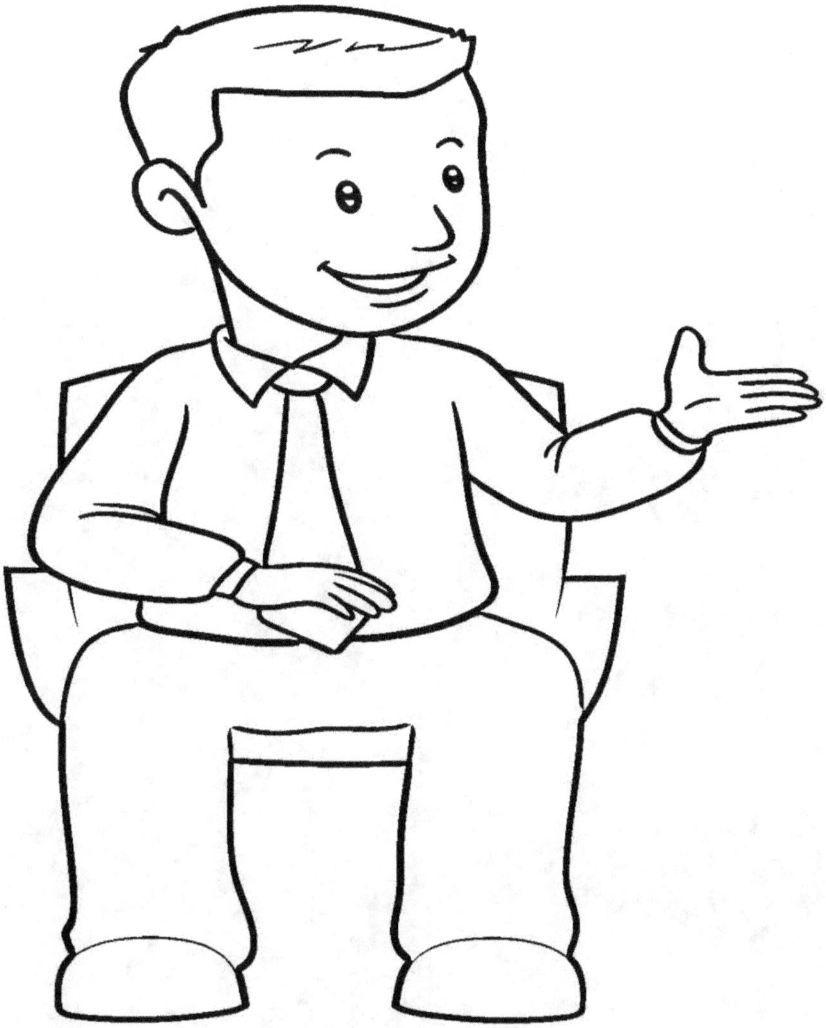

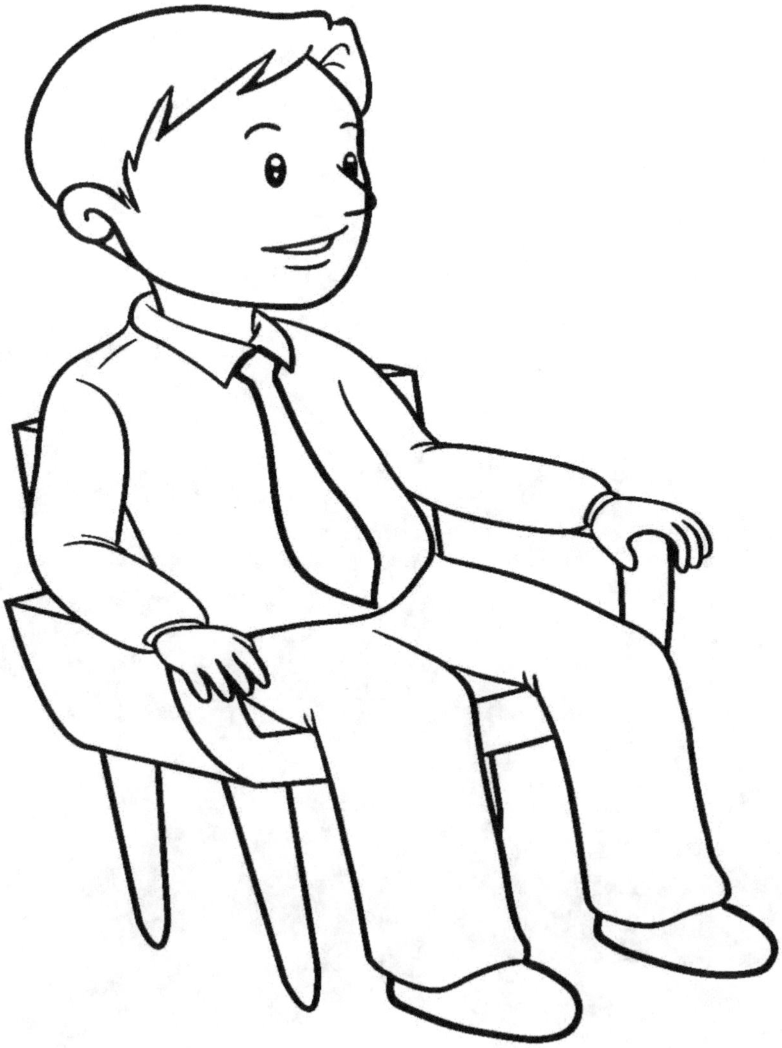

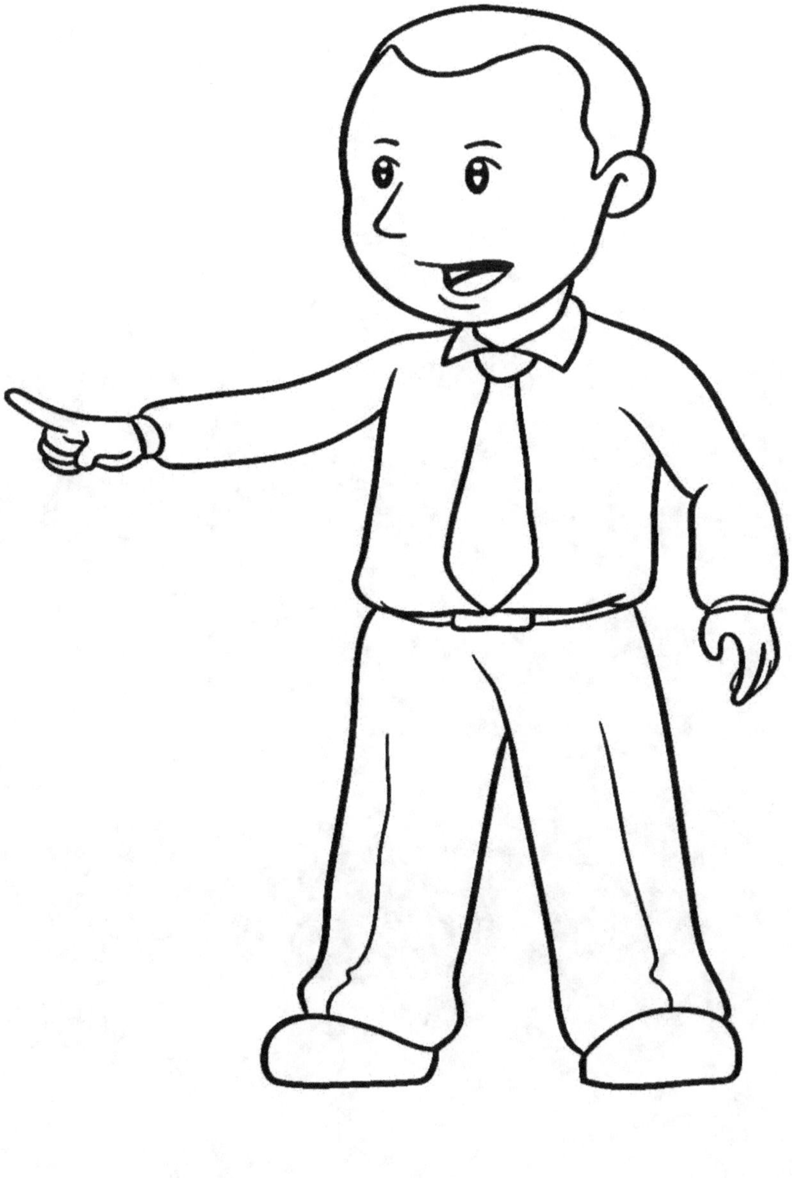

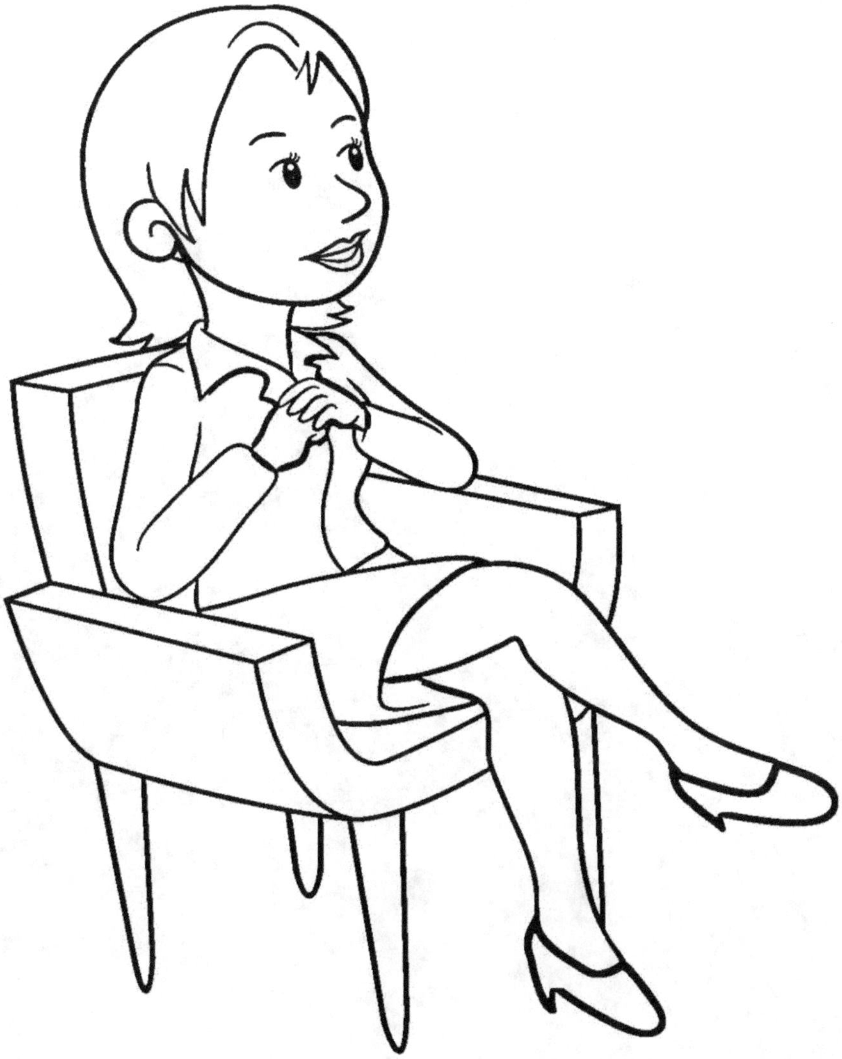

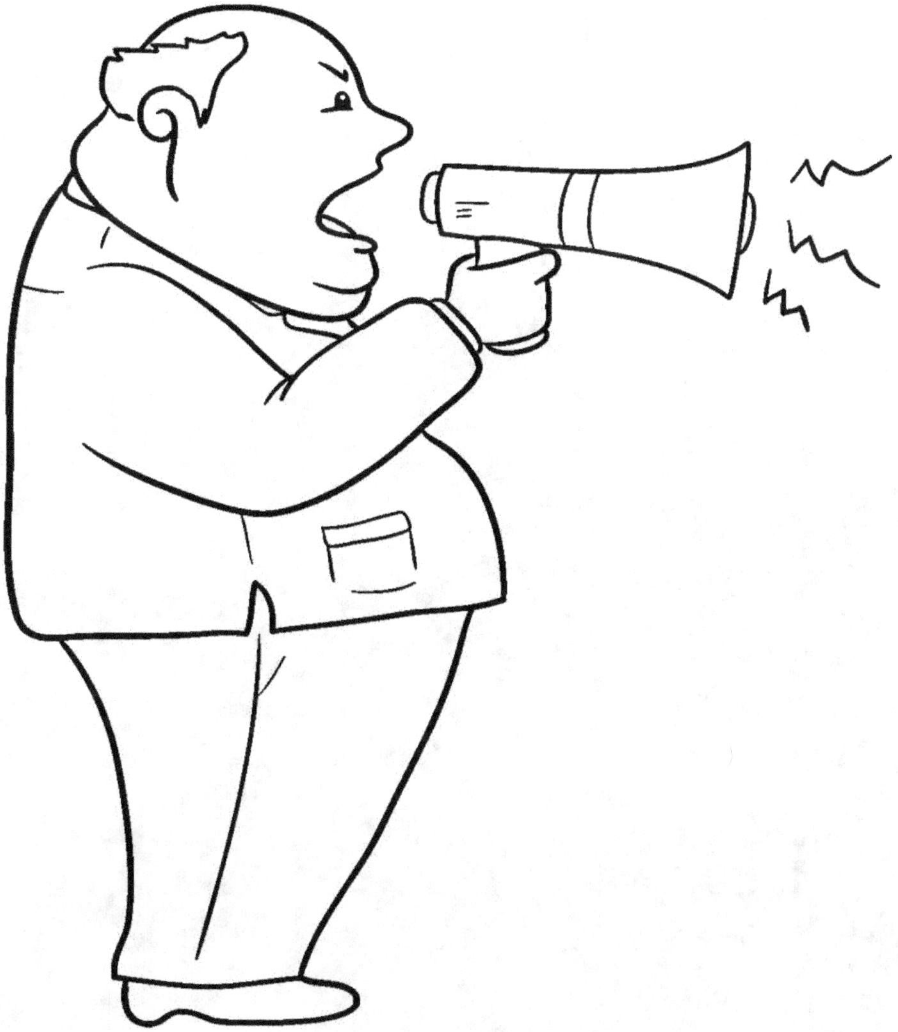

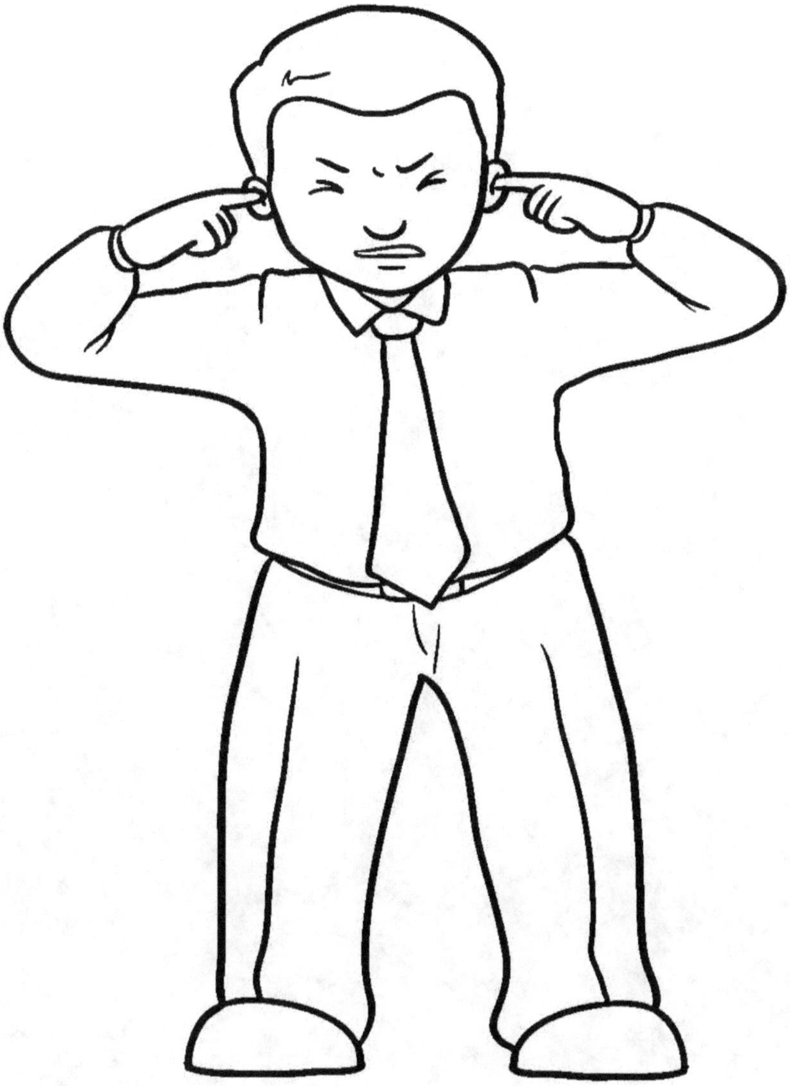

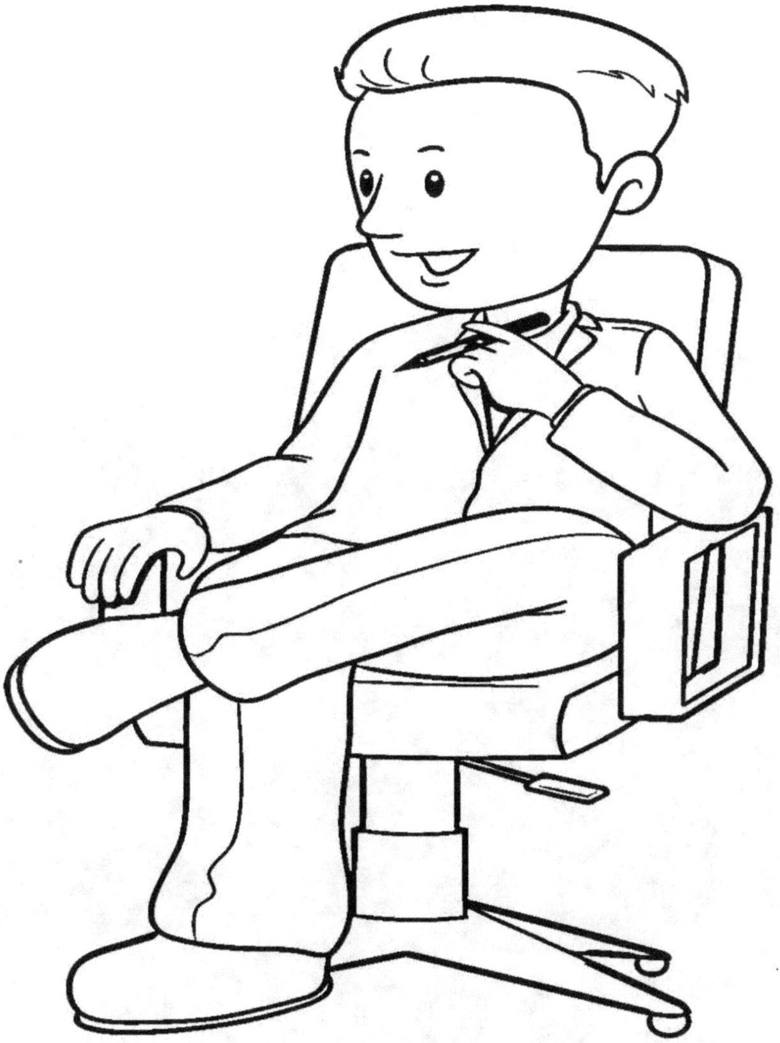

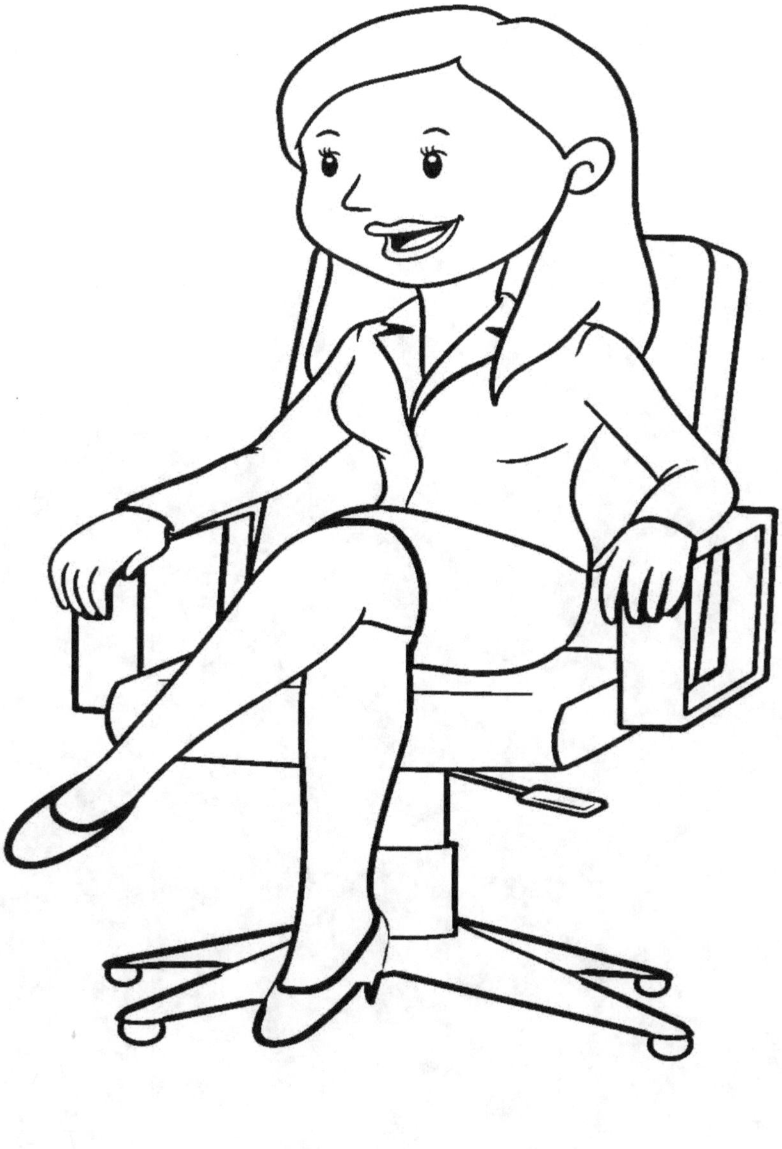

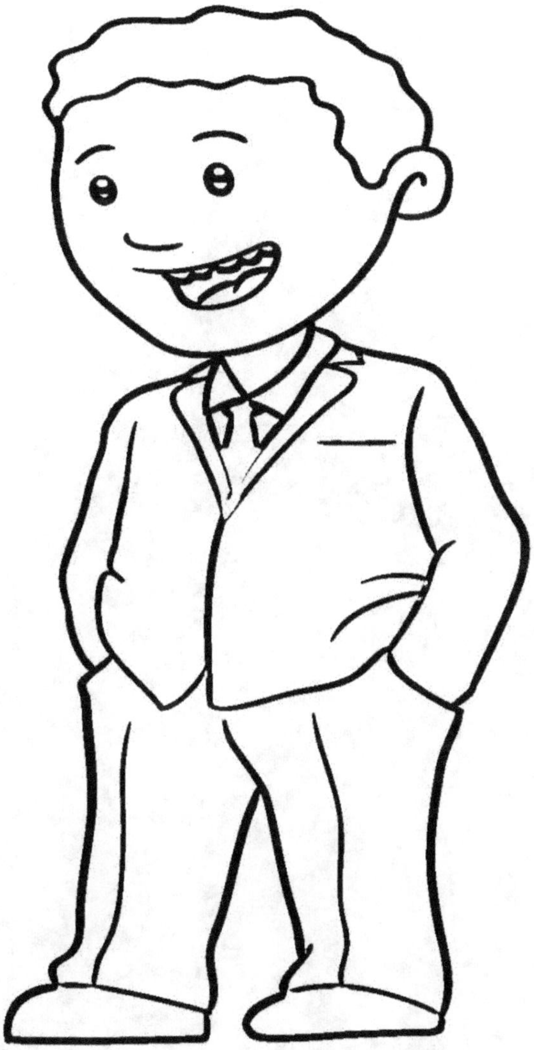

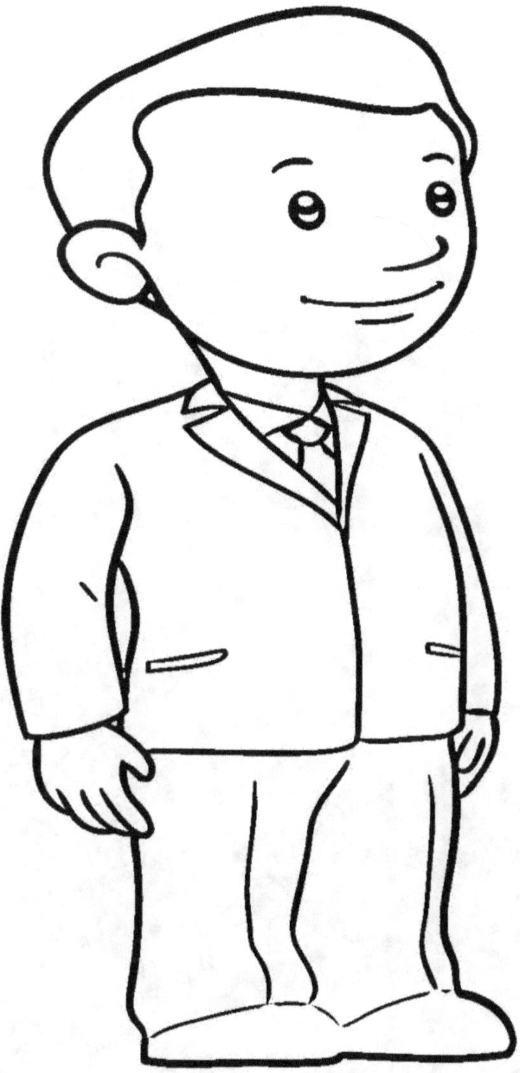

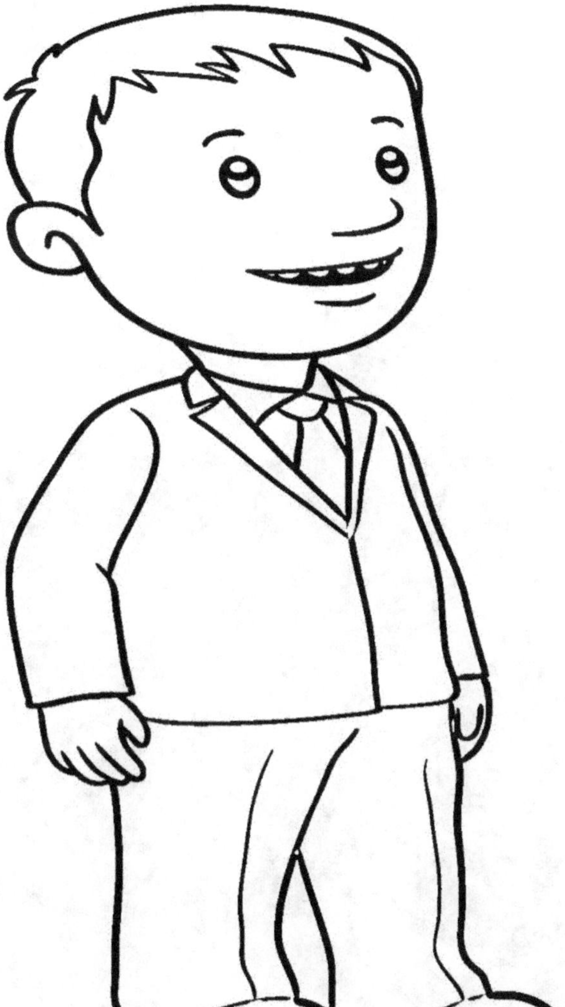

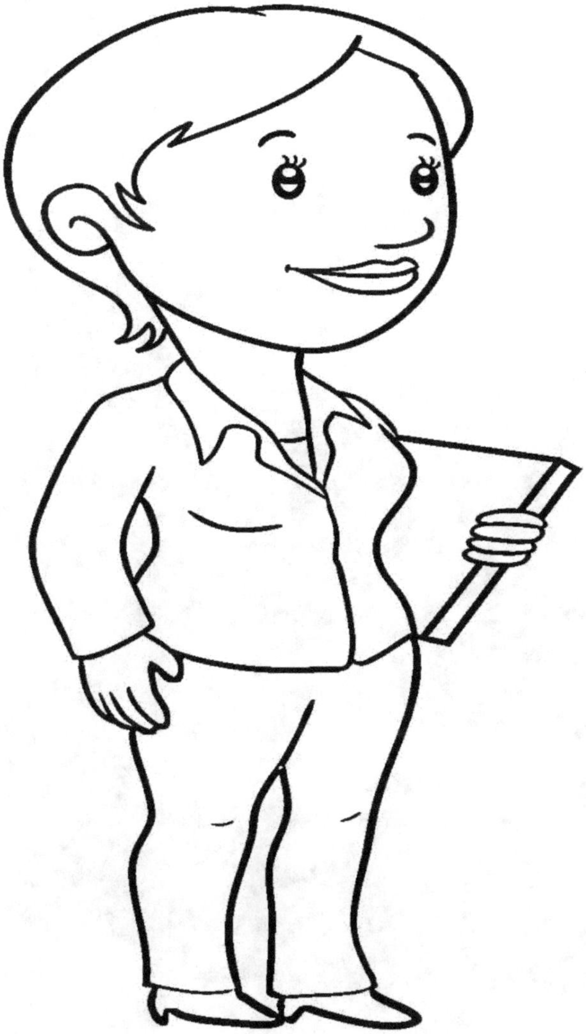

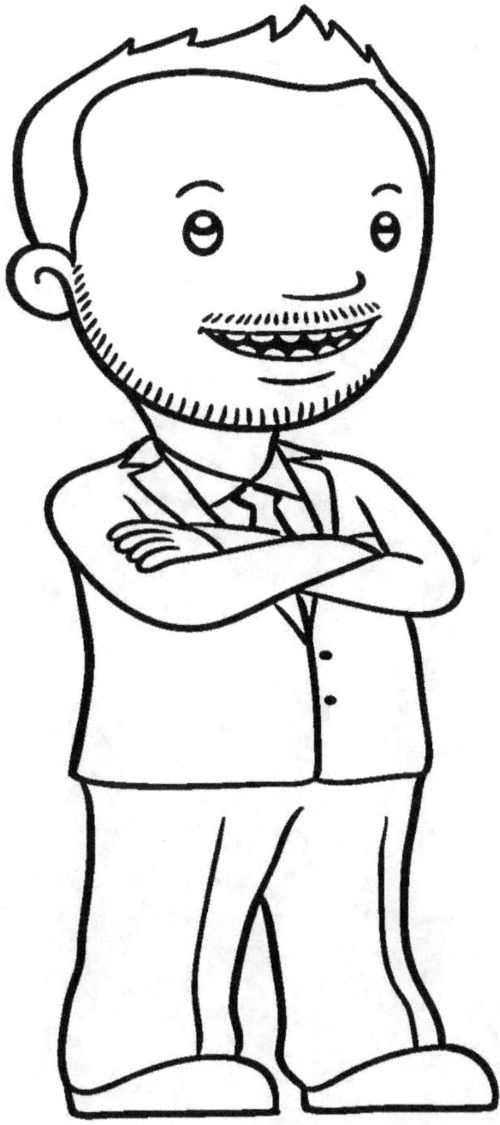

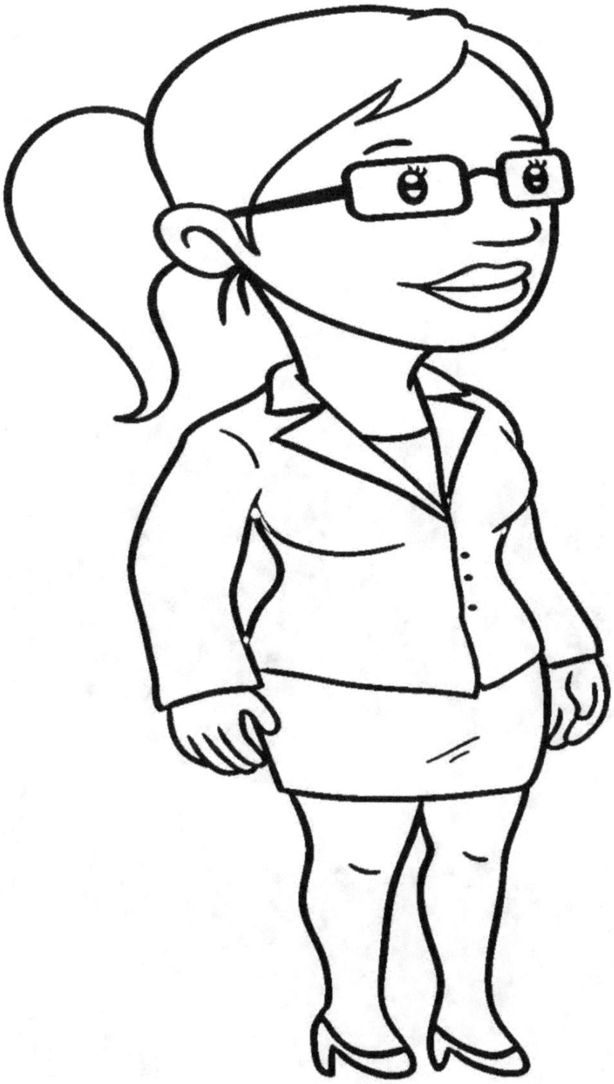

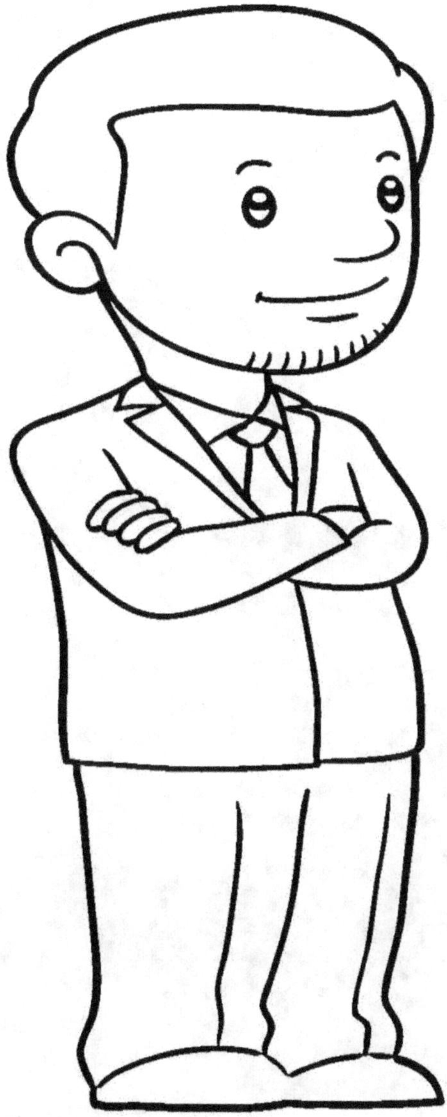

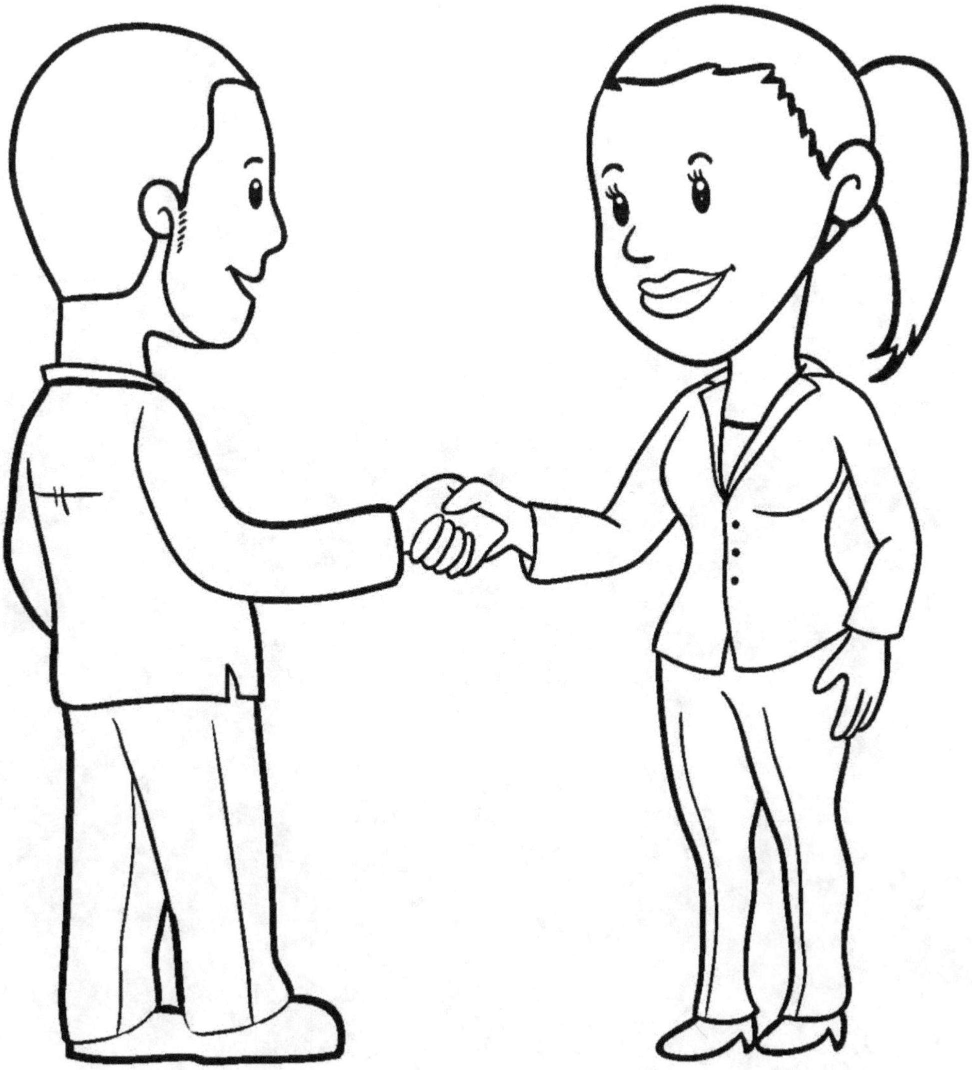

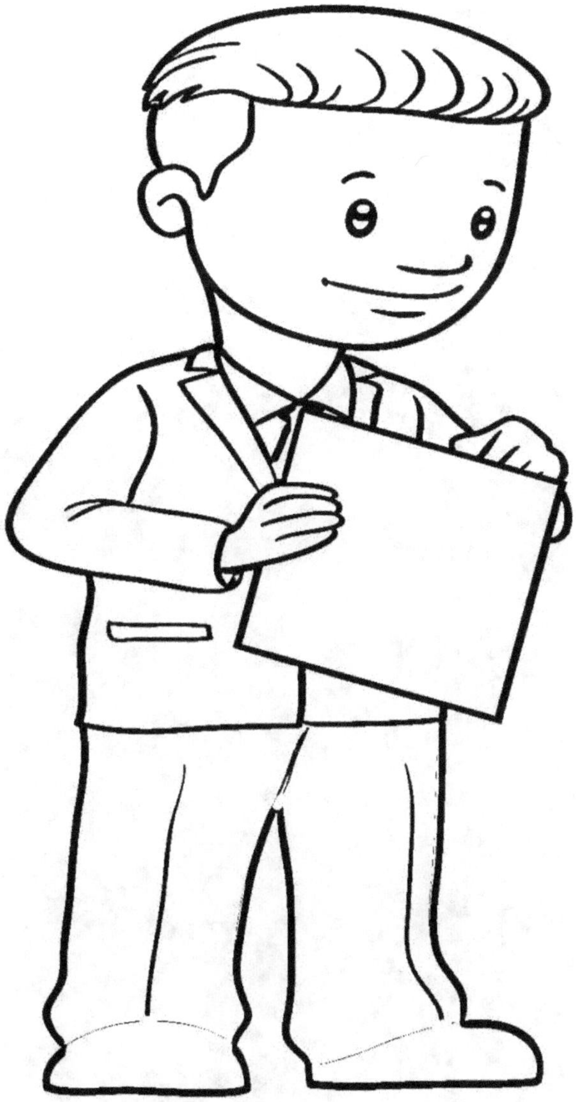

www.ingramcontent.com/pod-product-compliance
Lightning Source LLC
Chambersburg PA
CBHW081406170526
45166CB00010B/3231
9781519507976